C000171174

Google
Search
Poetry

transcribed by

nathan bragg

theresa vogrin

idiocratea

Idiocratea is an imprint of Polygon Publishing LTD.

POLYGON
PUBLISHING

www.polygonpublishing.com

www.idiocratea.com

ISBN-13: 978-1073695812

life is like google.
you just need to know
what you are
searching for.

contents

questions

where did i l|

where did i **leave my keys**

where did i **leave my wallet**

where did i **leave my glasses**

where did i **lose your love**

why isn't|

why isn't **prince philip king**

why isn't **wall street in jail**

why isn't **facebook working**

why isn't **insulin taken orally**

why isn't **pluto a planet anymore**

why isn't **11 pronounced onety one**

why must i

why must i **cry**

why must i **be a teenager in love**

why must i **be a crustacean in love**

why must i **chase the cat**

does your v|

does your v**oice sound different when recorded**

does your v**ote count**

does your v**ision change during pregnancy**

does your v**oice change when you lose weight**

does your v**irginity grow back**

what happens|

what happens **when**

what happens **when you die**

what happens **if**

what happens **in vegas**

what if w|

what if w**ild animals ate fast food**

what if w**e were made for each other**

what if w**e could**

what if w**e ruin it all and we love like fools**

I

why do|

why do **fools fall in love**

why do **we fall**

why do **i feel so sad**

why do **you smile**

is it a re|

is it a re**bound**

is it a re**lationship**

is it re**al diamond**

are there people who|

are there people who **look like me**

are there people who **never sleep**

are there people who **never find love**

are there people who **don't dream**

are there people who **are attracted to pokemon**

why can't i|

why can't i **cry**

why can't i **breathe**

why can't i **focus**

why can't i **pee**

why must we pr|

why must we pr**ay**

why must we pr**ay for our enemies**

why must we pr**aise god**

why must we pr**eheat the oven**

can you|

can you **run**

can you **feel the love tonight**

can you **freeze cheese**

perhaps i h|

perhaps i h**ad a wicked childhood**

perhaps i h**ave changed since then**

perhaps i h**ave the strength after all**

perhaps i h**ave a special anus**

could we a|

could we a**ll be dead**

could we a**ll be seeing different colours**

could we a**rrange a meeting**

could we a**t least stop at starbucks**

why are y|

why are y**ou my remedy**

why are y**ou leaving**

why are y**outube videos lagging**

why are y**ou wearing that stupid man suit**

I

how do i convert to|

how do i convert to **judaism**

how do i convert to **catholicism**

how do i convert to **islam**

how do i convert to **pdf**

why must you

why must you **hurt me in this way**

why must you **have a control**

why must you **operate the exhaust blower**

what is it|

what is it **like to die**

what is it **good for absolutely nothing**

what is it **like to be a bat**

why does t|

why does **the sun go on shining**

why does **the world exist**

why does **the queen have two birthdays**

why does **the internet hate anne hathaway**

did we t|

did we t**rain isis**

did we t**ake it too far**

did we t**urn clocks back**

why does |

why does **my eye twitch**

why does **it always rain on me**

why does **my poop float**

why does **god allow suffering**

why does **my computer keep freezing**

why does **the earth spin**

why does **my mom turn me on**

how to stop the gl|

how to stop the gl**are on my glasses**

how to stop the gl**itter from falling off clothing**

how to stop gl**obal warming**

is there a|

is there a **god**

is there a **meteor shower tonight**

is there a **santa claus**

is there a **ghost lyrics**

is there a**nybody out there**

is there a **cure for herpes**

where the hell are |

where the hell are **you**

where the hell are **my keys**

where the hell are **you when I need you**

where the hell are **my cheetos**

what would happen if|

what would happen if **the earth stopped spinning**

what would happen if **yellowstone erupted**

what would happen if **the sun went out**

what would happen if **there was no moon**

what would happen if **an asteroid hit earth**

what would happen if **a girl took viagra**

what would happen if **i hired two private investigators to follow each other**

what kind of|

what kind of **dog is boo**

what kind of **pill is this**

what kind of **dog should i get**

what kind of **cat do i have**

what kind of **asian are you**

or is|

or is **it just me**

or is **it a bagel**

or is **someone loving you**

or is **it just a one night stand**

is it healthy to

is it healthy to **fast**

is it healthy to **wash your hair every day**

is it healthy to **shave pubic hair**

is it healthy to **fart**

is it healthy to **cry**

is it healthy to **eat eggs every day**

is it healthy to **drink your own urine**

is it healthy to **eat boogers**

when will|

when will **the world end**

when will **i ovulate**

when will **i see you again**

when will **i be loved**

when will **i die**

statements

i feel like c|

i feel like **chicken tonight**

i feel like **crying**

i feel like **crap**

i don't d|

i don't d**eserve you**

i don't d**ance**

i don't d**rink**

i don't d**o drugs, i am drugs**

i e|

i endorse these strippers lyrics

i encompass and i eclipse

i exalt thee

i ejaculate fire

i've decided t|

i've decided to **stop wearing underwear**

i've decided to **marry you**

i've decided t**hat I'm great**

i don't v

i don't v**ote**

i don't v**omit from drinking**

i don't v**ote because**

i don't v**accinate my children**

i can see

i can see **clearly now**

i can see **russia from my house**

i can see **for miles**

i have lo|

i have lo**ved you for a thousand years**

i have lo**ved you with an everlasting love**

i have lo**ved to the point of madness**

i have lo**w self esteem**

i'm a h|

i'm a human not a sandwich

i'm a horrible person

i wish i knew|

i wish i knew **how it would feel to be free**

i wish i knew **how to quit you**

i wish i knew **then what i know now**

i wish i knew **natalie portman**

i eat|

i eat **cannibals**

i eat **donkey balls**

i eat **chalk**

i eat **even though I'm not hungry**

i hate it when i|

i hate it when i **lose my black friend in the dark**

i hate it when i **lose my white friends in the snow**

i hate it when i **lose**

i hate it when i**'m making a milkshake**

i hate it when i **forget to turn my swag off**

I

i stole a|

i stole a **loaf of bread**

i stole a **car**

i stole a **laptop**

i stole a **timelord**

i|

i **got high**

i **saw her face**

i **was guided**

i **took an arrow to the knee**

i just want

i just want **to ride bikes with you**

i just want **you to know who i am**

i just want **it all lyrics**

i just want **my pants back**

i want to

i want to **know what love is**

i want to **hold your hand**

i want to **scream and shout**

i want to **draw a cat for you**

i told her

i told her **i like her**

i told her **i like her now what**

i told her **i love her**

i told her **what time it was**

i told him i

i told him i **like him**

i told him i **love him**

i told him i **just wanted to be friends**

i told him i **have herpes**

i thought|

i thought **i loved you then**

i thought **hurricane season was over**

i thought **he walked on water**

i thought **of you today**

i wonder if w|

i wonder if we'll **smile in our coffins**

i wonder if w**oody and buzz ever met**

i wonder if we'll **always be together**

i want my w|

i want my w**idgets now**

i want my w**ish to come true**

i want my w**ater to break**

i want my w**ife to lose weight**

i am|

i am **bored**

i am **legend**

i am **a celebrity get me out of here**

i am **the walrus**

i am **pregnant**

i am **extremely terrified of chinese people**

i was

i was **wrong**

i was **out of control**

i wa**nt to look cheap**

i wa**nt to do what bunnies do**

i fel|

i fell **in love**

i fell **asleep**

i fell **in love with you**

i felt **a funeral in my brain**

i was el|

i was elected to lead not to read

i was elected to end wars

i was electrocuted

i was elated

i was once |

i was once **like you are now**

i was once **like you**

i was once **possibly a cowboy king**

i was once **in darkness**

i slept |

i slept **for 3 hours**

i slept **with your mom**

i slept **well**

i saw |

i saw **the devil**

i saw **her standing there**

i saw **mommy kissing santa claus**

i wanted the|

i wanted the **whole world or nothing**

i wanted the **opposite of this**

i wanted the **world to be in uniform**

i wanted the **cashmere**

i'm always going to|

i'm always going to **be alone**

i'm always going to **love you**

i'm always going to **the toilet**

answers

you are |

you are **my sunshine**

you are **a pirate**

you are **the worst**

you are **always on my mind**

he told me

he told me **he likes me**

he told me **i give good head**

he told me **he loves me**

he told me **to move on**

one of you

one of you **will betray me**

one of you **turds**

get out|

get out**ta your mind**

get out **of debt**

get out **alive**

science is |

science is **awesome**

science is **fun**

science is **a liar sometimes**

some monsters|

some monsters **are different**

some monsters **die and others return**

some monsters **can be real friends**

my cat |

my cat **hates you**

my cat **lyrics**

my cat **carl**

my cat **loki**

my cat **says hello**

my cat **bites**

my cat **died last night**

my cat **looks like hitler**

we'll have |

we'll have **halloween on christmas**

we'll have **to muddle through somehow**

we'll have **a good time then**

we'll have **fun fun fun**

never put |

never put **a healthy dog down**

never put **a sock in a toaster**

never put **a blanket over an owl**

never put **it in writing**

never put **new shoes on a table**

never put **on weight**

never put **your banana in the refrigerator**

never put **baby in a corner**

at least i

at least i **got my friends**

at least i **tried**

at least i **can bhop**

at least i **have chicken**

I

sometimes when i'm alone|

sometimes when i'm alone **i cry**

sometimes when i'm alone **i google myself**

sometimes when i'm alone **i wonder**

sometimes when i'm alone **i pretend i'm a carrot**

it's time to |

it's time to **begin isn't it**

it's time to **stop posting**

it's time to **say goodbye**

it's time to **duel**

it's time to **party**

it's time to **move on**

it's time to **make the donuts**

there are things|

there are things **you don't know**

there are things **known and things unknown**

there are things **of which i may not speak**

there are things **i have done**

my heart isn't

my heart isn't **in it**

my heart isn't **broken**

my heart isn't **beating**

my heart isn't **a toy quotes**

in this be|

in this be**d i scream**

in this be**autiful world**

in this be**st of all possible worlds**

get me my |

get me my **files**

get me my **brown pants**

get me my **money**

get me my **angry wig**

my brother |

my brother **the wind**

my brother **is an italian plumber**

my brother **the devil**

my brother **my captain my king**

and |

and **i love her**

and **the snakes start to sing**

and **the mountains echoed**

and **we danced**

those are

those are**n't muskets**

those are**n't pillows**

those are **people who died**

those are **balls**

nicolas cage is

nicolas cage is **god**

nicolas cage is **a vampire**

nicolas cage is **crazy**

nicolas cage is **everyone**

smile today t |

smile today **thunderbird**

smile today **tomorrow could be worse**

he was s

he was s**at or he was sitting**

he was s**aying goodbye to his horse**

he was s**taring at me**

he was s**o cool**

somehow you|

somehow you **and i collide**

somehow you **needed me**

somehow you **left me neglected**

somehow you **seem so alive**

I

the years go|

the years go **fast and the days go slow**

the years go **by**

the years go **fast and the days go so slow**

the years go **by like stones under rushing water**

the children are u|

my children are u**nhappy**

my children are u**ngrateful**

my children are u**.s. citizens**

my children are u**gly**

google is |

google is **your friend**

google is **watching you**

google is **hiring**

google is **making us stupid**

google is **crap**

google is **evil**

if you enjoyed *Google Search Poetry*
please consider leaving a review
on amazon.

thank you.

other books published by *idiocratea*:

overheard at waitrose
overheard at waitrose II
overheard at whole foods
milk and brexit

about this book

Google Search Poetry is a collection of the most iconic poems found through search engines and posted across social media platforms like twitter, facebook and instagram.

idiocratea doesn't hold the copyright to the words, only to the presentation of them. this book is not authorised, endorsed by or affiliated with *Google* or its subsidiaries.

our only intention with this book is to make people laugh and brighten up their day.

about *idiocratea*

idiocratea is an imprint of Polygon Publishing LTD. with our constantly expanding selection of trendy mugs, meme related products, gag gifts, personalised items and our very own range of original books, we at *idiocratea* pride ourselves on selling extraordinary gifts for extraordinary people.

check us out on instagram (*@idiocratea_* and *@polygon.publishing*) and don't forget to browse our stores at **www.idiocratea.com** and **www.polygonpublishing.com**.

about the contributors

nathan bragg

nathan bragg is a uk-based digital marketing specialist, entrepreneur and lover of memes.

theresa vogrin

theresa vogrin is an austrian writer, living in the uk. she published her debut poetry book *Bitter-Sweet* in july 2018.

check out theresa's work on instagram (*@theresa_vogrin*) and facebook.